Explode The Code® 2nd Edition

Teacher's Guide for Books 1 and 2

Nancy Hall

EDUCATORS PUBLISHING SERVICE
Cambridge and Toronto

Printed in Benton Harbor, MI, in February 2019
ISBN 978-0-8388-7815-6

5 PPG 19

Introduction

Explode The Code (ETC) provides a time-tested approach to teaching phonics. *ETC* breaks down the learning of phonic elements into manageable chunks so that children continually feel success as they move through the program.

Based on the Orton-Gillingham technique, *ETC* is equally suitable for one-on-one instruction and group or whole-class instruction. A clearly established routine helps provide students with a "road map" through each lesson, so learning a new set of instructions never interferes with learning new skills. The instruction is straightforward and sensible. (See Lesson Routine at a Glance in the inside front cover.) *Explode The Code* is designed to be used with other ELA materials, such as literature and decodable readers. For a variety of appropriate EPS decodable readers, both print and eBooks, see eps.schoolspecialty.com/products/literacy/decodable-readers.

Systematic, Direct Teaching of Phonics

Jeanne Chall's *Learning to Read: The Great Debate*—an extensive review of classroom, laboratory, and clinical research—revealed the efficacy of a direct, explicit, systematic teaching of decoding skills. Chall concluded that code emphasis programs produced better results, "not only in terms of the mechanical aspects of literacy alone, as was once supposed, but also in terms of the ultimate goals of reading instruction—comprehension and possibly even speed of reading" (Chall 1967, 307).

Even as new understandings about learning and teaching have evolved in the years since 1967, these findings have been repeatedly reconfirmed (Bond and Dykstra 1967; Chall 1983; Adams 1990; National Reading Panel 2000). In 2000, the National Reading Panel presented its findings of studies published since 1970, comparing phonics instruction with other kinds of instruction. Focusing on kindergarten through sixth grade, the panel concluded that systematic phonics instruction enhanced children's ability to read, spell, and comprehend text, particularly in the younger grades. These results were especially evident in the word-reading skills of disabled readers and children from low socioeconomic backgrounds, and in the spelling skills of good readers.

Chall and Popp write of "two kinds of meaning—meaning of the medium (the print) and the meaning of the message (the ideas)" (1996, 2). Knowledge of phonics gives students the ability to decode print, which in turn reveals the message ideas. The more words early readers can recognize, the more accessible meaning becomes. Children who have difficulty identifying words lack the fluency needed to concentrate on meaning (Rasinsky 2000). Conversely, children who are given direct, systematic instruction in decoding skills have the tools for developing fluent, meaningful reading. Furthermore, they have the tools to produce print and consequently express their thoughts in writing, which in turn reinforces their word identification skills (Ehri, 1998).

While the place of direct, systematic phonics in the teaching of reading has changed throughout the years, one thing has always been true: Children need to "break the code"—the sound-symbol correlation—in order to decode and comprehend what they read. And while a small percentage of children can do this partly or mostly on their own, the overwhelming majority of children need direct instruction, with some needing intervention and more practice.

Explode The Code offers a complete systematic phonics program for the elementary grades. Phonetic elements and patterns, carefully sequenced to consider both frequency of use and difficulty, are presented in sequence and practiced in a series of instructive workbooks. Teacher's Guides accompany all the books.

The recent Common Core State Standards initiative has been a controversial one, but the section known as the "Foundational Skills" is perhaps the least controversial, as it merely restates the need for skills students have long been known to require in order to be successful readers: For example, the Foundational Skills say:

"These standards are directed toward fostering students' understanding and working knowledge of concepts of print, the alphabetic principle, and other basic conventions of the English writing system. <u>These foundational skills are not an end in and of themselves; rather, they are necessary and important components of an effective, comprehensive reading program designed to develop proficient readers with the capacity to comprehend texts across a range of types and disciplines.</u> [emphasis ours] *Instruction should be differentiated: good readers will need much less practice with these concepts than struggling readers will."*
(CCSSI, 15)

The CCSS go on to provide signposts along the way to literacy that differ little from the Scope and Sequences of skills provided within most any phonics program.

The first three books of the *Explode The Code* series—Books A, B, and C—focus on visual identification of consonants, their written lowercase forms, and their sound–symbol relationships. An engaging, colorful wall chart with felt objects representing key words for the twenty-six letters of the alphabet may be used to introduce children to the names and sounds of the lowercase letters and/or to reinforce lessons in books A, B, and C. An activity book with instructions for thirty-five games comes with the wall chart. Key word picture–letter cards are also available for Books A, B, and C, while Code Cards reinforce and review the letter sounds taught in Books 1–3 ½.

The remaining eight books—*Explode The Code* Books 1 through 8—progress through the vowel sounds and patterns, consonant clusters and digraphs, syllables, and suffixes. A pretest at the beginning of Book 1 helps teachers ensure that students are ready for work with these phonic elements. Posttests are found at the end of each workbook. If these show that extra practice is needed, additional workbooks, from 1½ to 6½, provide this extra practice in the same skills as the matching whole number book. Posttests at the end of these "half" books will ensure that children are ready to progress to the next level. A separate criterion-referenced Placement Test is available to assess the specific phonic concepts children know and those they need to be taught.

Through systematic direct teaching of phonics using *Explode The Code*, the following successes in reading and writing occur:

- The alphabetic principle is firmly established.
- Phonological awareness skills are fostered alongside the phonics teaching.
- Understanding of how sound–symbol relationships permit words and text to be decoded and encoded is fully developed and practiced, enhancing fluency and automaticity.
- Students of varying language and skill needs are accommodated through vocabulary and concept building, exposure to differing approaches to teaching phonics, and flexible grouping and use of the materials.
- See more about the research for this series at http://epsbooks.com.

References

Adams, M.J. (1990). *Beginning to Read: Thinking and Learning about Print.* Cambridge, MA: MIT Press.

Bond, G. & Dykstra, R. (1967). "The cooperative research program in first grade reading." *Reading Research Quarterly* 2: 5–142.

Chall, J.S. (1967, 1983). *Learning to Read: The Great Debate.* New York: McGraw-Hill.

Chall, J.S. & Popp, H.M. (1996). *Teaching and Assessing Phonics, Why, What, When, How: A Guide for Teachers.* Cambridge, MA: Educators Publishing Service.

Common Core State Standards Initiative. (2010) *Common Core State Standards for English Language Arts & Literacy in History/Social Studies, Science, and Technical Subjects.* Washington, DC, National Governors Association Center for Best Practices and the Council of Chief State School Officers.

Ehri, L.C. (1998). "Grapheme–phoneme knowledge is essential for learning to read words in English." In: Metsala, J.L. & Ehri, L.C. (eds.) *Word Recognition in Beginning Literacy.* Mahway, NJ: Erlbaum, 3–40.

National Reading Panel (2000). *Teaching Children to Read: An Evidence Based Assessment of the Scientific Research Literature on Reading and Its Implication for Reading Instruction: Reports of the Subgroups.* Washington: National Institute of Child Health and Development.

Rasinsky, T.V. (2000). "Does speed matter in reading?" *The Reading Teacher* 54:146–151.

Explode The Code Books 1 and 2 Teacher's Guide and Key

Explode The Code Teacher's Guides expand on the skills presented in the student books, providing teachers with various options for instruction and reinforcement. The guides address the principles of phonemic awareness, phonics, vocabulary, fluency, and comprehension as they relate to each new skill presented in the lesson. They also include suggestions for writing practice and differentiating instruction. Each lesson follows the same easy-to-use format:

Quick Review   Each new lesson begins with a review of previously learned concepts or sound-symbol relationships.

Phonological/Phonemic Awareness   This section provides instruction to help students recognize and manipulate the sounds in spoken words. Struggling learners may need this kind of support on an ongoing basis in order to improve their ability to read and spell. The oral activities in this section help students focus on and work with the sounds of words in the lesson. The activities in Books 1 and 2 focus on blending and segmenting phonemes in words. Other activities ask students to identify, isolate, or manipulate phonemes.

Phonics   This section helps students learn the sound–symbol relationships necessary for decoding words. Teachers introduce each skill by calling attention to sounds in familiar words. Then they teach students the letter or letters that represent that sound. Students then practice the skill, working with other words that include that phonic element.

Vocabulary   Learning new words is essential to the development of reading comprehension. This section defines unfamiliar words from the lesson. It also identifies the sight words necessary for completing the exercises.

Completing Student Pages   This section directs the class to the corresponding *Explode The Code* student books. Teachers read the student book directions with the class and check for understanding of the task. They identify any unfamiliar illustrations and walk through a sample item on each page. Each student book lesson follows a predictable format; as students learn the format, they should be able to complete the pages without further assistance.

Comprehension   In order for students to fully understand what they read, they need to be able to use, discuss, define, and understand words in a variety of ways. The comprehension-building activities in this section expand students' understanding of lesson words and concepts by having them answer questions, use words in oral sentences, explain the meaning of words in context, and draw pictures. Students can then apply their word comprehension skills to a variety of texts.

Fluency   Fluent readers spend less time decoding words and give more attention to comprehending text. In this section, a variety of fluency activities help students develop skills in reading sentences and passages accurately and quickly. The rotating menu of fluency-building activities includes the following: choral and echo reading, word automaticity, noting punctuation, developing or improving accuracy, reading with expression, reading dialogue, improving rate, and phrasing.

Writing   Writing goes hand-in-hand with phonics instruction. In this section, students practice writing words from the lesson. Activities include writing answers to word clues, copying sentences, writing dictated sentences, and writing original sentences.

Differentiating Instruction   The rotating menu of activities in this section provides suggestions accommodating a broad range of learning needs and styles. ELL tips and activities help teachers identify and accommodate potential problem areas for English language learners. Extra Practice refers teachers to lessons in Books 1½ and 2½ that can be used for extra practice. Challenge activities are provided for students who complete the student book pages without difficulty. Learning Styles activities address the learning styles of kinesthetic, visual/spatial, auditory, musical, or linguistic learners. Computer-based Reinforcement activities direct teachers to *ETC Online*, where students can get additional practice with *Explode The Code* phonics skills in an interactive, dynamic format.

Key   Answers to the posttests for Books 1, 1½, 2, and 2½ are provided.

Explode The Code Coordinating Materials

Explode The Code **Placement Test**   The tests in this quick assessment help teachers determine student placement within the *Explode The Code* series.

Ready, Set, Go **Picture–Letter Cards**   The *Ready, Set, Go* Picture Letter Cards feature initial consonants taught in Books A, B, and C. The set consists of twenty-one sheets, each with a picture card, a letter card, and a picture card with the letter superimposed.

Wall Chart and Activity Book   The *Explode The Code* Wall Chart is a colorful felt wall chart with letter pockets containing tangible felt objects that reinforce the key words for the twenty-six letters of the alphabet and their sounds. The Activity Book for the Wall Chart provides ideas for several activities and games to further aid in learning the names and sounds of the letters taught in Books A, B, C, and 1.

Explode The Code **Code Cards**   This set of fifty-four index cards reinforces the sound–symbol relationships taught in *Explode The Code* Books 1–3. Code Cards can be used for instruction and review.

Explode The Code **for English Language Learners**   This resource supplements instruction of *Explode The Code* Books 1–3 by providing specific direction for teachers of English language learners. Reproducible student pages are included.

Explode The Code **Extra Practice Books**   *Explode The Code* Books 1½–6½ provide further practice in the skills taught in Books 1–6.

Beyond The Code   The *Beyond The Code* books provide opportunities for advanced reading of longer stories. These books incorporate skills from the *Explode The Code* books, introduce many more sight words, and emphasize reading comprehension and critical thinking.

ETC Online   *ETC Online* presents the *Explode The Code* content in an interactive and dynamic format. *ETC Online's* adaptive technology adjusts the content it delivers automatically, according to the student's performance. It has extensive feedback features for students, parents, teachers, and administrators. See www.explodethecode.com for details.

Book 1

Consonant Pretest

Have students turn to page i. Tell students to look at the letter at the beginning of the line and ◯ (circle) the picture that begins with the same sound. Identify pictures if necessary. Have students complete pages i–iii independently.

Students who miss five or more items on this Pretest may not be ready to go on to new material and should instead complete *Explode The Code* Books A, B, and C at this time. Students who miss fewer than five items are ready for Book 1. Notice which letters, if any, were missed and incorporate them into review.

Lesson 1
Short *a* with final *t*

Materials: *Ready, Set, Go* Picture-Letter Cards; *Explode The Code* Code Card 1

Quick Review

Review the consonants using consonant cards from the *Ready Set Go* Picture-Letter Cards. Ask students to give the letter, the letter sound, and the name of the key word for each consonant. Tell students that today they will learn about a vowel sound.

Phonemic Awareness

Phoneme Blending   Tell students you are going to sound out some words very slowly. Ask students to listen to the sounds, repeat the sounds, and say the word. For example, ask, What word is /s/ /a/ /t/? Response: /s/ /a/ /t/ is *sat*.

/r/ /a/ /t/ (rat)
/f/ /a/ /t/ (fat)
/p/ /a/ /t/ (pat)
/b/ /a/ /t/ (bat)
/h/ /a/ /t/ (hat)
/m/ /a/ /t/ (mat)

Phonics

Introduce the Skill   Show students an apple or a picture of an apple and ask them to name it. Ask students what sound they hear at the beginning of *apple.* (/ă/) Ask students if anyone can name the letter that makes the /ă/ sound. (*a*)

Write the letter *a* on a chart or display Code Card 1. Have students repeat the rule after you: *a says /a/ as in apple.* Have students brainstorm other words that begin with the sound /a/.

Tell students that they may hear the /ă/ sound at the beginning of some words and also in the middle of words like *mat, sat, bag,* and *ham.* Have students brainstorm additional words with the middle sound /ă/. Display some of these words, sounding each letter out as you write it. Then ask volunteers to underline the letter *a* in each word.

Vocabulary

Introduce New Vocabulary   If students are not familiar with lesson words or concepts, provide explanations such as the following: An **astronaut** is a person who flies rockets into space. A **mat** is a small rug. A **bat** is a mammal with wings. To **add** means to combine numbers together.

Introduce Sight Words   Introduce the new sight words used in the lesson: *on, the,* and *is.* Read the words to the class. Have them think up sentences using this word. Then have them write the letters in the air using their fingers as a pencil. Add the sight words to the Word Wall and have students add the word to their personal dictionaries.

Completing Student Pages 1–9

Read the directions with students. Identify any pictures that may be unfamiliar, such as *rake, anchor,* and *alligator* on page 1. Together, complete a sample item on each page. Then have students complete the pages independently, providing assistance as needed.

Fluency

Word Automaticity   Provide or have students create several flashcards with *-at* words. Have students flip through the cards as they read the words to a partner. Encourage students to review the flashcards multiple times as they work to increase their accuracy and speed.

Comprehension

Extending Word Knowledge   Ask questions or give directions such as the following to be sure that students understand short-*a* words used in this lesson:

1. Can a **bat** have wings? (yes)
2. Can you use a **bat** to hit a ball? (yes)
3. Show me how you would **pat** a dog.
4. Would a **rat** be a friend to a **cat**? (no)
5. Name some different kinds of **hats**. (baseball, cowboy, straw, wool)

Writing   Display the words *sat, cat, mat, hat,* and *rat.* Have students write numbers 1–5 on sheets of lined paper. Tell them to choose and write the word that matches each clue you say.

1. This animal is like a mouse. (rat)
2. You wear this on your head. (hat)
3. Before you go inside, you might wipe your feet on this. (mat)
4. This is a pet. (cat)
5. Today you sit, but yesterday you _____. (sat)

Differentiating Instruction

Learning Styles (Kinesthetic)   Have kinesthetic learners use letter tiles to build new *-at* words by substituting initial consonant letters. Have students say each new word they form and write it on a piece of paper or a white board.

Challenge   Write *at* and *bat* on the board and have students make up oral sentences using these words. Continue with *rat* and *sat,* then with *cat* and *hat.*

ELL   Spanish does not contain some of the short vowel sounds found in English. See *Explode The Code for English Language Learners* for additional work with short vowels.

Computer-based Reinforcement   Give students additional practice with short *a* with final *t* on *ETC Online,* Units 1.1.2 to 1.1.7.

Lesson 2

Short *a* with final *n, m, d, t*

Materials: a soft cloth ball; *Explode The Code* Code Card 1;
Explode The Code Wall Chart

Quick Review

Play a game of toss as you review the sounds of short *a* and the consonants. Toss a soft ball to a student as you say a letter sound. Have the student who catches the ball name the letter that makes that sound and provide the key word: *n* says /n/ as in *nest.* Then have the student return the ball. Repeat these sounds randomly until everyone has had a turn. Repeat short *a* every second or third throw. Display the Wall Chart nearby to remind the class of the key words.

Phonemic Awareness

Phoneme Isolation   Ask students to tell you the last sound in the following words: *can, fat, ham, bad, ran, mat,* and *ram.* (/n/, /t/, /m/, /d/, /n/, /t/, /m/)

Phonics

Review the Skill   Ask the class to tell you what sound short *a* makes. (/ă/) Remind them that in Lesson 1 they learned a lot of short-*a* words that ended with the letter *t.* Write *bat* on the board. Tell students that today they are going to learn some short-*a* words that end with other letters. Write *ban* below *bat.* Sound out the letters and ask what the word is. Continue with *bad.* Ask students to brainstorm some other words that end in -*an,* -*ad,* or -*am* and write the words on the board as you sound them out.

Vocabulary

Introduce New Vocabulary   If students are not familiar with lesson words or concepts, provide explanations such as the following: A **lad** is a little boy.

Introduce Sight Words   Introduce the new sight words used in the lesson: *has* and *in.* Read each word to the class. Have students think of sentences using each word. Then have them write the letters in the air using their fingers as a pencil. Add the sight words to the Word Wall or have students add them to their personal dictionaries.

Completing Student Pages 10–17

Read the directions with students. Identify any pictures that may be unfamiliar, such as *Pam* for the name of the girl in row 4 and *hut* in row 5 on page 12; and the *man* in row 2 on page 13. Together, complete a sample item on each page. Then have students complete the pages independently, providing assistance as needed.

Fluency

Developing Accuracy   Have students take turns rereading the sentences on page 16 with the person sitting next to them. Instruct students to monitor each other for accuracy.

Comprehension

Extending Word Knowledge   Ask questions or give directions such as the following to be sure that students understand short-*a* words used in this lesson:

1. What is another word for mad? (angry)
2. Describe what a traffic jam might look like. (lots of cars on the road, not moving)
3. What is another word for sad? (unhappy, upset)
4. What is the opposite of Dad? (Mom)
5. Sometimes people who like sports a lot are called fans. Are you a fan of something?

Writing   Display the words *sad, ran, bad, pan,* and *mad.* Have students write numbers 1–5 on sheets of lined paper. Tell them to choose and write the word that matches each clue you say.

1. This means the opposite of good. (bad)
2. You might fry an egg in this. (pan)
3. Today I run, but yesterday I ____. (ran)
4. What is another word for angry? (mad)
5. What is opposite of happy? (sad)

Differentiating Instruction

Learning Styles (Auditory)   Have auditory learners think of some words that rhyme with *can.* As students think of words, write them on the board. When you have a good collection, ask the class to read the words aloud in unison. Then ask them to provide some oral sentences or rhymes using these words, for example, *The man ran.*

Computer-based Reinforcement   Give students additional practice with short *a* with final *n, m, d,* and *t* on *ETC Online,* Units 1.2.1 to 1.2.7.

Lesson 3

Short *a* with final consonants

Materials: *Explode The Code* Code Card 1; *Explode The Code* Wall Chart

Quick Review

Tell students to listen to the sound at the *end* of each word you say. Have volunteers say the ending sound, and have the other students indicate their agreement or disagreement with thumbs up or thumbs down: *pat, Sam, pan, dad, bat, pad, Pam,* and *can.*

Phonemic Awareness

Phoneme Blending   Tell students you are going to sound out some words very slowly. Ask students to listen to the sounds, repeat the sounds, and say the word. For example, ask, What word is /r/ /a/ /g/? Response: /r/ /a/ /g/ is *rag.*

/m/ /a/ /p/ (map)
/b/ /a/ /g/ (bag)
/f/ /a/ /n/ (fan)
/p/ /a/ /l/ (pal)
/c/ /a/ /p/ (cap)
/h/ /a/ /d/ (had)
/c/ /a/ /n/ (can)
/g/ /a/ /s/ (gas)

Phonics

Review the Skill   Show the class Code Card 1. Ask them to name the letter, the sound, and the key word for short *a*. Pass around the card and the apple from the Wall Chart (or a real apple) as students repeat the phrase: *a* says /ă/ as in *apple.*

Vocabulary

Introduce New Vocabulary   If students are not familiar with lesson words or concepts, provide explanations such as the following: A **tag** is a card attached to something as a label, like a **tag** on something you buy tells you the price. **Sap** is a sticky substance that comes from trees and is used to make syrup. **Pal** is another word for friend. **Cap** is another word for **hat**. A **bass** is a kind of fish.

Completing the Student Pages 18–25

Read the directions with students. Identify any pictures that may be unfamiliar, such as *pass* in row 1 and *sap* in row 2 on page 22. Together, complete a sample item on each page. Then have students complete the pages independently, providing assistance as needed.

Fluency

Word Automaticity   Provide or have students create several flashcards with *-an, -am, -ad, -at, -ap,* and *-ag* words. Have students flip through the cards as they read the words to a partner. Encourage students to review the flashcards multiple times as they work to increase their accuracy and speed. Include cards from previous lessons as review.

Comprehension

Extending Word Knowledge   Ask questions or give directions such as the following to be sure that students understand short-*a* words used in this lesson:

1. A dog wags its tail. Show what it means for something to wag.
2. When something sags, it droops. Show how your shoulders might sag.
3. Who are your pals? What kinds of things do you do with your pals?
4. The words *Sam, Jan, Pat, Al, Pam, Dan,* and *Nat* are all what? (names) Do you know anyone with one of those names?
5. When would you want to have a map with you? (when you are in an unfamiliar place)

Writing   Display the words *hat, nap, tag, gas,* and *map.* Have students write numbers 1–5 on a sheet of lined paper. Tell them to choose and write the word that matches each clue.

1. You wear this on your head. (hat)
2. When you are sleepy you take a ____. (nap)
3. This helps you figure out where you are or where you want to go. (map)
4. This is a game where you might say, "You're it!" (tag)
5. A car needs this to run. (gas)

Differentiating Instruction

Learning Style (Kinesthetic)   Kinesthetic learners will benefit from using letter tiles to build words from the lesson. Have students build new words by replacing the beginning consonant in the word families *-ap (tap, nap, cap, lap, sap)* and *-ag (bag, tag, wag, lag).* Have students say each new word they form and write it on a piece of paper or a white board.

Extra Practice   Find more practice with short *a* in *Explode The Code* Book 1½, Lesson 1.

Challenge   Have students think of two rhyming short-*a* words to answer the following clues:

1. This is an unhappy parent. (sad dad)
2. This is a chubby mouse relative. (fat rat)
3. This could be a hat you wear when you take a short rest. (nap cap)
4. This is a sack that holds little pieces of paper. (tag bag)

Computer-based Reinforcement   Give students additional practice with short *a* with final consonants on *ETC Online,* Units 1.3.1 to 1.3.7.

Lesson 4
Short *i*

Materials: *Explode The Code* Code Card 2;
Explode The Code Wall Chart

Quick Review

To review, have students blend onsets and rimes and tell you what word you are saying. Then ask them to spell the word aloud.

/k/ . . . ap (cap, c-a-p)
/t/ . . . ap (tap, t-a-p)
/p/ . . . an (pan, p-a-n)
/m/ . . . an (man, m-a-n)
/j/ . . . am (jam, j-a-m)
/s/ . . . am (Sam, s-a-m)

Phonemic Awareness

Phoneme Segmentation   Have students break each word into its separate sounds, saying each sound as they tap it out or count it.

it: /ĭ/ /t/ (2 sounds)
sit: /s/ /ĭ/ /t/ (3 sounds)
dim: /d/ /ĭ/ /m/ (3 sounds)
hip: /h/ /ĭ/ /p/ (3 sounds)
in: /ĭ/ /n/ (2 sounds)
bin: /b/ /ĭ/ /n/ (3 sounds)
pig: /p/ /ĭ/ /g/ (3 sounds)

Phonics

Introduce the Skill   Show students the Wall Chart igloo or a picture of an igloo and ask them to name the picture. Ask students what sound they hear at the beginning of *igloo*. (/ĭ/) Ask students if anyone can name the letter that makes the /ĭ/ sound. (*i*)

Write the letter *i* on a chart or display Code Card 2. Have students repeat the rule after you: *i* says /ĭ/ as in *igloo*. Have students brainstorm other words that begin with the sound /ĭ/.

Tell students that they may hear the /ĭ/ sound at the beginning of some words and also in the middle of words like *sit, dip, pig,* and *Tim*. Have students brainstorm additional words with the middle sound /ĭ/. Display some of these words, sounding each letter out as you write it. Then ask volunteers to underline the letter *i* in each word.

Vocabulary

Introduce New Vocabulary   If students are not familiar with lesson words or concepts, provide explanations such as the following: An **inch** is about this long (demonstrate). People sometimes measure objects in **inches**. An **itch** is a tingling feeling that makes you want to scratch it. A **wig** is a covering of hair for people's heads. A **fin** is part of a fish.

Completing Student Pages 26–34

Read the directions with students. Identify any pictures that may be unfamiliar, such as *wagon* in item 2 on page 26; or *hill* in row 2 on page 29. Together, complete a sample item on each page. Then have students complete the pages independently, providing assistance as needed.

Fluency

Word Automaticity   Give each pair of students a set of cards with several short-*i* words from the lesson. Have them stack the cards faced down and turn over one card one a time. Tell students to try to read the word together as soon as they turn it over. If they do not say the same word, have them check the word in their books, if needed, and read it together again.

Comprehension

Extending Word Knowledge   Ask questions or give directions such as the following to be sure that students understand short-*i* words used in this lesson:

1. What is shorter, a hill or a mountain? (hill)
2. Name some animals with fins. (fish, sharks)
3. Big is the opposite of small. What is the opposite of short? (tall)
   The opposite of soft? (hard)
4. If you come in first place in a race, you don't lose, you ____. (win)
5. If you gulp something, you drink it quickly.
   What is a word that means drink slowly? (sip)

Writing   Display the words *dig, mitt, pig, fin,* and *sit.* Have students write numbers 1–5 on sheets of lined paper. Tell them to choose and write the word that matches each clue you give.

1. This animal says *oink* and likes the mud. (pig)
2. This is the opposite of *stand.* (sit)
3. This will help a fish swim through the water. (fin)
4. You use a shovel to do this. (dig)
5. You use this to catch a softball or baseball. (mitt)

Differentiating Instruction

ELL   In Spanish the letter *i* makes the sound of long *e*. Note this possible confusion and provide students with extra practice as necessary. See *Explode The Code for English Language Learners* for more work with short *i*.

Learning Styles (Auditory)   Have auditory learners think of some words that rhyme with *zip.* As students think of words, write them on the board. When you have a good collection, ask the class to read them aloud together. Then ask them to provide some oral sentences or rhymes using these words, for example, *Kip takes a sip.*

Extra Practice   Find more practice with short *i* in *Explode The Code* Book 1½, Lesson 2.

Computer-based Reinforcement   Give students additional practice with short *i* on *ETC Online,* Units 1.4.1 to 1.4.7.

Lesson 5
Review Lesson: short *a* and *i*

Materials: a soft cloth ball; *Explode The Code* Wall Chart

Quick Review

Play a game of toss as you review the sounds of short *a* and *i, v, w, x, y,* and *z.* Toss a soft ball to a student as you say a letter sound. Have the student who catches the ball name the letter that makes that sound and provide the key word: *y* says /y/ as in *yarn.* Then have the student return the ball. Repeat these sounds randomly until everyone has had a turn. Repeat short *a* or *i* every second or third throw. Display the Wall Chart nearby to remind the class of the key words.

Phonemic Awareness

Phoneme Isolation   Have students tell you what vowel sound (/ă/ or /ĭ/) they hear in each word: *cap, dig, bit, sag, bat, fit, gas, had,* and *lip.*

Phonics

Skill Review   Say a three-letter word from Lessons 1–4. Display two letters of the word, leaving a blank line for the missing letter. Have a volunteer fill in the missing letter, spell the word aloud, and read the word to the class.

Vocabulary

Introduce New Vocabulary   If students are not familiar with lesson words or concepts, provide explanations such as the following: A **bib** protects a baby's clothes while the baby eats. A **lid** is a covering, or top, for a container.

Completing Student Pages 35–41

Read the directions with students. Identify any pictures that may be unfamiliar, such as *shop* in row 3 on page 35. Together, complete a sample item on each page. Then have students complete the pages independently, providing assistance as needed.

Fluency

Repeated Reading   Write the following sentences on the board. Point to each sentence as you read it aloud to the class. Have the class echo-read it as you point to each word. Then reread all three sentences together:

1. The pan hit the man.
2. The pig sits on a hill.
3. Tim sat on the big mat.

Comprehension

Write words from Lessons 1–5 on individual cards. Have students pick two cards without looking at them and then make up an oral sentence using the words on the cards. Repeat until all cards have been selected.

Writing   Have students choose and copy two sentences from the fluency exercise above onto lined paper. Remind them to use capital letters and periods.

Differentiating Instruction

Extra Practice   Find more practice with short *a* and *i* in Lesson 3 of *Explode The Code* Book 1½.

Challenge   Have students make a word chain by changing one letter in a word to form a new short-*a* or short-*i* word. For example, have students start with the word *cat*. Tell them to change one letter to make a new word and write that word under *cat*. (*cap*) Then have them continue to change one letter to make a new word (*nap* to *nip* to *tip* to *tap*). Challenge students to come up with a long chain of real words.

Learning Styles (Visual/Kinesthetic)   Create word card sets with these words: *bad, sap, sip, did, can, bin, dig, ham, sat, hid, cap, Dan, din, cat, sit, him, had, hat,* and *dim.* Have students sort the cards three times: first by short vowel, next by first letter, and then by final letter. Have them read each new group of words.

Computer-based Reinforcement   Give students additional practice with short *a* and short *i* review on *ETC Online,* Units 1.5.1 to 1.5.6.

Lesson 6
Short *u*

Materials: *Explode The Code* Code Cards 1–3, *Explode The Code* Wall Chart

Quick Review
Make sure that every student has Code Cards 1 and 2 (or index cards with *a* and *i*). Ask students to listen for the sound they hear in the *middle* of each word. As they do, have them show the letter card that matches the sound: *fin, fan, mat, mitt, win, tin, tan,* and *bit.*

Phonemic Awareness
Phoneme Blending   Tell students you are going to sound out some words very slowly. Ask students to listen to the sounds, repeat the sounds, and say the word. For example, ask, What word is /c/ /u/ /p/? Response: /c/ /u/ /p/ is *cup.*

/f/ /u/ /n/ (fun)
/m/ /u/ /d/ (mud)
/r/ /u/ /n/ (run)
/h/ /u/ /m/ (hum)
/l/ /u/ /k/ (luck)
/b/ /u/ /d/ (bud)

Phonics
Introduce the Skill   Show students the Wall Chart umbrella or a picture of an umbrella and ask them to name it. Ask students what sound they hear at the beginning of *umbrella.* (/ŭ/) Ask students if anyone can name the letter that makes the /ŭ/ sound. (*u*)

Write the letter *u* on a chart or display Code Card 3. Have students repeat the rule after you: *u* says /ŭ/ as in *umbrella.* Have students brainstorm other words that begin with the sound /ŭ/.

Tell students that they may hear the /ŭ/ sound at the beginning of some words and also in the middle of words like *run, nut, cut,* and *hum.* Have students brainstorm additional words with the middle sound /ŭ/. Display some of these words, sounding each letter out as you write it. Then ask volunteers to underline the letter *u* in each word.

Vocabulary

Introduce New Vocabulary   If students are not familiar with lesson words or concepts, provide explanations such as the following: A **sub** is an underwater boat. A **tug** is a type of boat that pulls other boats. When you **tug** something, you pull it. A **hut** is a small house.

Completing Student Pages 42–50

Read the directions with students. Identify any pictures that may be unfamiliar, such as *under* in rows 2 and 4 and *upside down* in row 3 on page 42; and *hug* in row 1 on page 44. Together, complete a sample item on each page. Then have students complete the pages independently, providing assistance as needed.

Fluency

Developing Accuracy   Have students take turns rereading the sentences on page 49 with the person sitting next to them. Instruct students to monitor each other for accuracy.

Comprehension

Extending Word Knowledge   Ask questions or give directions such as the following to be sure that students understand short-*u* words used in this lesson:

1. What is the difference between a mug and a cup?
   (appearance, type of beverage each holds)
2. Name as many kinds of nuts as you can.
   (peanut, walnut, cashew, almond, hazelnut)
3. Name as many kinds of bugs as you can. (ants, spiders, fleas, etc.)
4. A pup is a baby dog. What is a baby cat? (kitten) A baby cow? (calf)
   A baby horse? (colt)
5. What do you get when you add water to dirt? (mud)

Writing   Have students write numbers 1–5 on sheets of lined paper. Tell them to write the short-*u* word from the lesson that matches each clue:

1. This is a short word meaning "insect." (bug)
2. Some students ride this big, yellow vehicle to school. (bus)
3. This is the opposite of *walk.* (run)
4. The moon shines at night. What shines during the day? (sun)
5. This is a kind of underwater boat. (sub)

Differentiating Instruction

Learning Styles (Visual)   Have students fold a piece of paper in half. Have them draw and label a **bug** on the top half and a **sun** on the bottom. Then have students write the words *rug, hug, dug, mug,* and *tug* around the bug and the words *run, bun,* and *fun* around the sun. Have them underline the *ug* or *un* in each word.

Extra Practice   Find more practice with short *u* in Lesson 4 of *Explode The Code* Book 1½. Find more practice with short *u* and short *i* in Lesson 5 of *Explode The Code* Book 1½.

Computer-based Reinforcement   Give students additional practice with short *u* on *ETC Online*, Units 1.6.1 to 1.6.7.

Lesson 7

Review Lesson: short *a, i,* and *u*

Materials: a soft cloth or foam ball

Quick Review

Play a game of toss as you review the sounds of short *a, i,* and *u*. Toss a soft ball to a student as you say a letter sound. Have the student who catches the ball name the letter that makes that sound and provide the key word: *i* says /ĭ/ as in *igloo*. Then have the student return the ball. Repeat these sounds randomly until everyone has had a turn.

Phonemic Awareness

Have students tell you the sound they hear in the *middle* of each of these words: *pup, bad, bit, gum, sap, hip, tab, pin, bus, dad, win,* and *cap*.

Phonics

Skill Review   Say a three-letter word from Lessons 1–6. Display two letters of the word, leaving a blank line for the missing letter. Have a volunteer fill in the missing letter, spell the word aloud, and read the word to the class.

Vocabulary

Review Vocabulary Words   Review vocabulary words from Lessons 1–6 as necessary.

Introduce Sight Words   Introduce the new sight words used in the lesson: *to, I, yes, no, or,* and *and.* Read the words to the class. Have them think of sentences using each word. Then have them write the letters in the air using their fingers as a pencil. Add the sight words to the Word Wall and have students add them to their personal dictionaries.

Completing Student Pages 51–58

Read the directions with students. Identify any pictures that may be unfamiliar, such as *fill* in row 2, *bun* in row 4, and *mug* in row 5 on page 52. Together, complete a sample item on each page. Then have students complete the pages independently, providing assistance as needed.

Fluency

Repeated Reading   Display the following sentences on the board or distribute copies to each student. Point to each sentence and read it aloud to the class. Have the class echo it by reading it back to you. Then reread all three sentences together.

1. The big bug hugs the rug.
2. The mitt fits Matt.
3. Gus has the gas can.

Comprehension

Write words from Lessons 1–6 on individual cards. Have students pick two cards without looking at them and then make up an oral sentence using the words on the cards. Repeat until all cards have been selected.

Writing   Have students copy the sentences from the fluency exercise above onto lined sheets of paper. Remind them to use capital letters and periods.

Differentiating Instruction

Extra Practice   Find more practice with short *a, i,* and *u* in Lesson 6 of *Explode The Code* Book 1½.

Learning Styles (Auditory)   Have auditory learners think of some words that rhyme with *jug* (or any other short *u, a,* or *i* word). As students think of words, write them on the board. When you have a good collection, ask the class to read them aloud together. Then ask them to provide some oral sentences or rhymes using these words, for example, *the bug dug.*

Computer-based Reinforcement   Give students additional practice with short *a,* short *i,* and short *u* review on *ETC Online,* Units 1.7.1 to 1.7.6.

Lesson 8
Short *e*

Materials: *Explode the Code* Code Cards 1–4

Quick Review

Remind students that they have already learned about short vowel sounds for the letters *a, i,* and *u.* Write the letters or display Code Cards 1, 2, and 3. Ask volunteers to name the letters, tell which short vowel sounds they represent, and name the key words.

For a cumulative review, make sure every student has Code Cards 1–3 or three index cards with the letters *a, i,* and *u.* Ask the class to listen for the sound they hear in the middle of the following words and show the letter card that matches the sound: *bud, bad, bid, nut, bun, ban, fun, bug, fan, fin, big,* and *bag.*

Phonemic Awareness

Phoneme Blending   Tell students you are going to sound out some words very slowly. Ask students to listen to the sounds, repeat the sounds, and say the word. For example, ask, What word is /b/ /e/ /g/? Response: /b/ /e/ /g/ is *beg.*

/p/ /e/ /n/ (pen)
/g/ /e/ /t/ (get)
/b/ /e/ /t/ (bet)
/r/ /e/ /d/ (red)
/w /e/ /t/ (wet)
/m/ /e/ /n/ (men)
/l/ /e/ /g/ (leg)

Phonics

Introduce the Skill   Show students a picture of an egg and ask them to name the picture. Ask students what sound they hear at the beginning of *egg.* (/ĕ/) Ask students if anyone can name the letter that makes the /ĕ/ sound. (e)

Write the letter *e* on a chart or display Code Card 4. Have students repeat the rule after you: *e* says /ĕ/ as in *egg.* Have students brainstorm other words that begin with the sound /ĕ/.

Tell students that they may hear the /ĕ/ sound at the beginning of some words and also in the middle of words like *met, peg, ten,* and *set.* Have students brainstorm additional words with the middle sound /ĕ/. Display some of these words, sounding out each letter as you write it. Then ask volunteers to underline the letter *e* in each word.

Vocabulary

Introduce New Vocabulary   If students are not familiar with lesson words or concepts, provide explanations such as the following: An **elf** is a make-believe character that they might read about in a fairy tale. **Elves** are like small people who sometimes play tricks.

Completing the Student Pages 59–67

Read the directions with students. Identify any pictures that may be unfamiliar, such as *elf* in row 1 on page 59, *net* in row 3 on page 64, and *mess* in row 1 on page 65. Together, complete a sample item on each page. Then have students complete the pages independently, providing assistance as needed.

Fluency

Word Automaticity   Give each pair of students a set of cards with several words from the lesson. Have them stack the cards face down and turn over one card at a time. Tell students to try to read the word together as soon as they turn over the card. If they do not say the same word, have them check the word in their books, if needed, and read it together again.

Comprehension

Extending Word Knowledge   Ask questions or give directions such as the following to be sure that students understand short *e* words used in Lesson 8:

1. Does a **bed** have **legs**? How many? (yes, four)
2. Show me **ten** fingers.
3. What does a **hen** lay? (eggs)
4. What can you catch in a **net**? (fish, butterflies)
5. Name something that is **red**. (apple, wagon, car, strawberry, fire engine)

Writing   Have students write numbers 1–5 on sheets of lined paper. Tell them to write a three-letter short-e word that matches each clue you give:

1. An apple is often this color. (red)
2. This has ink and you can write with it. (pen)
3. This part of your body is attached to your foot. (leg)
4. A dog or cat that belongs to somebody is a _____? (pet)
5. This has a mattress and you sleep on it. (bed)

Differentiating Instruction
ELL In Spanish the letter *e* makes a vowel sound similar to the English long-*a* sound. Note this possible confusion as native Spanish speakers read short-*e* words. See *Explode The Code for English Language Learners* for more work with short *e*.

Learning Styles If students have difficulty distinguishing between /e/ and other short vowel sounds, have them hold their fingers lightly around their chins. Tell them to listen and feel where their chin is when they say these sounds: /a/, /i/, /u/, /e/. Then use the sounds in words and have students point their thumbs up or thumbs down to indicate when they hear short *e* as you say *pan, pun, pin, pen,* etc.

Challenge Have students write the following headings lengthwise across a piece of paper: *-et, -ed, -en, -ell,* and *-eg*. Ask them to think of as many words as they can to write under each heading. Answers may include the following sets of words:

    met, set, get, net
    red, Ted, fed, led, bed
    pen, ten, men, hen, den, Jen
    well, bell, tell, sell, fell, yell
    leg, peg, beg, Meg

Computer-based Reinforcement Give students additional practice with short *e* on *ETC Online,* Units 1.8.1 to 1.8.7.

Lesson 9
Review of short *a, i, u, e*

Materials: *Ready, Set, Go* Picture-Letter Cards *v, w, x, y, z;*
Explode the Code Code Cards 1–4; *Explode the Code* Wall Chart

Quick Review
Using the cards listed above, have students take turns naming the letters, pronouncing the sounds, and naming the key words. Use the felt objects from the Wall Chart for the key words if needed as a hint.

Phonemic Awareness

Tell students you are going to sound out some words very slowly. Ask students to listen to the sounds, repeat the sounds, and say the words:

/l/ /i/ /p/
/j/ /u/ /g/
/m /e/ /t/
/c/ /u/ /t/
/f/ /e/ /d/
/s/ /i/ /x/
/t/ /e/ /n/
/r/ /e/ /d/

Then have students name the sound they hear in the *middle* of each of these words: *six, ten, did, bun, vet, map, fed, bell, kin,* and *Gus.*

Phonics

Skill Review   Play "Word Chain" with the class. Write the word *cat* on the board. Have a volunteer change one letter to make a new word and write that word below, for example, *cap.* Continue and see how many words students can come up with. (Example of a word chain: *map, mat, cat, can, pan, pen, pet, set, sat, bat, but, bug, tug.*) Provide clues or start a new word chain as necessary.

Vocabulary

Introduce New Vocabulary   If students are not familiar with lesson words or concepts, provide explanations such as the following: A **hip** is the joint that joins your leg to the rest of your body.

Introduce Sight Words   Introduce the new sight word used in the lesson: *his.* Read the word to the class. Have them think up sentences using this word. Then have them write the letters in the air using their fingers as a pencil. Add the sight word to the Word Wall and have students add the word to their personal dictionaries.

Completing Student Pages 68–75

Read the directions with students. Identify any pictures that may be unfamiliar, such as *tip* in row 1 and *beg* in row 4 on page 70; *hid* in row 6 and *zip* in row 7 on page 71; and *set* on row 4 on page 73. Together, complete a sample item on each page. Then have students complete the pages independently, providing assistance as needed.

Fluency

Echo Reading   Write the following sentences on the board. Point to the each sentence and read it aloud to the class. Have the class echo it by reading it back to you. Then reread all three sentences together.

1. The bell fell in the well.
2. Ben's pet is wet.
3. Bud begs for a bag of nuts.

Comprehension

Write words from Lessons 1–9 on individual cards. Have students pick two cards without looking at them and then make up an oral sentence using the words on the cards. Repeat until all cards have been selected.

Writing   Have students choose and copy two sentences from the fluency exercise above onto sheets of lined paper. Remind them to use capital letters and periods.

Differentiating Instruction
Extra Practice   Find more practice with short *a, i, e,* and *u* in Lesson 8 of *Explode The Code* Book 1½.

Learning Style (Auditory)   Divide the class into four or five equal groups. Give each group one short *a, i, e,* or *u* word (for example, *net*) and tell them to come up with rhyming words (*pet, let, get, yet, and met*). Ask each group to tell you their words and write them on the board.

Computer-based Reinforcement   Give students additional practice with short *a*, short *i*, short *u*, and short *e* on *ETC Online*, Units 1.9.1 to 1.9.7.

Lesson 10

Short *o*

Materials: a soft ball, *Explode The Code* Code Card 5,
Explode The Code Wall Chart (octopus)

Quick Review

Play a game of toss as you review the sounds of short *a, i, e,* and *u.* Toss a soft ball to a student as you say a letter sound. Have the student who catches the ball name the letter that makes that sound and provide the key word: for example, *e* says /ĕ/ as in *egg.* Then have the student return the ball. Repeat these sounds randomly until everyone has had a turn.

Phonemic Awareness

Phoneme Segmentation   Have students break each word into its separate sounds, saying each sound as they tap it out or count it:

on: /o/ /n/ (2 sounds)
pot: /p/ /o/ /t/ (3 sounds)
off: /o/ /f/ (2 sounds)
hot: /h/ /o/ /t/ (3 sounds)
bog: /b/ /o/ /g/ (3 sounds
mom: /m/ /o/ /m/ (3 sounds)

Phonics

Introduce the Skill   Show students the Wall Chart octopus or a picture of an octopus and ask them to name it. Ask students what sound they hear at the beginning of *octopus*. (/ŏ/) Ask students if anyone can name the letter that makes the /ŏ/ sound. (o)

Write the letter *o* on a chart or display Code Card 5. Have students repeat the rule after you: *o* says /ŏ/ as in *octopus*. Have students brainstorm other words that begin with the sound /o/.

Tell students that they may hear the /ŏ/ sound at the beginning of some words and also in the middle of words like *not, dog, hop,* and *Bob.* Have students brainstorm additional words with the middle sound /ŏ/. Display some of these words, sounding each letter out as you write it. Then ask volunteers to underline the letter *o* in each word.

Vocabulary

Introduce New Vocabulary   If students are not familiar with lesson words or concepts, provide explanations such as the following: **Fog** is made up of thick clouds that hang close to the ground. **Cop** is a slang word for a police officer. **Hog** is another word for a pig.

Completing Student Pages 76–84

Read the directions with students. Identify any pictures that may be unfamiliar, such as the *ostrich* in row 3 on page 76; and *log* in row 1 and *top* in row 5 on page 79. Together, complete a sample item on each page. Then have students complete the pages independently, providing assistance as needed.

Fluency

Word Automaticity   Provide or have students create several flashcards with short-*o* words from the lesson. Have students flip through the cards as they read the words to a partner. Encourage students to review the flashcards multiple times as they work to increase their accuracy and speed.

Comprehension

Extending Word Knowledge   Ask questions or give directions such as the following to be sure that students understand short-*o* words from the lesson.

1. Name the kinds of **jobs** you do in your classroom.
   (feeding plants, handing out snack)
2. Show how a **hop** can be different from a jump.
3. Explain how a curtain **rod** and a fishing **rod** are similar.
   Explain how they are different. (They are both straight, long poles. One is used to hang curtains, and the other is used with a reel and a fishing line to catch fish.)

Writing   Have students write numbers 1-5 on sheets of lined paper. Tell them to write a three-letter short-*o* word from the lesson that matches each clue you give:

1. This is a name for a piece of wood that you might put on a campfire. (log)
2. What is the opposite of bottom? (top)
3. If you work, you have a ____. (job)
4. You might use this to clean up a spill. (mop)
5. If you bounce up and down over and over, you ____. (hop)

Differentiating Instruction

ELL   In Spanish, the letter *a* makes a sound similar to the English short *o*. Note this possible confusion as native Spanish speakers sound-spell short-*o* words.

Learning Style (Kinesthetic)   Write all vowels and a selection of consonants on large, individual cards and give each student a card. Say a three-letter, short-vowel word (for example, *dot*). Tell students to look at their letter cards and come to the front of the room if they are holding a card with a letter that is in the word *dot*. Ask the three students to spell the word *dot* by standing in the correct order, and ask the rest of the class if they have spelled the word correctly. Repeat with other short-vowel words.

Extra Practice   Find more practice with short *o* in *Explode The Code* Book 1½, Lesson 9. Find more practice with short *o* and *e* in *Explode The Code* Book 1½, Lesson 10.

Computer-based Reinforcement   Give students additional practice with short *o* on *ETC Online,* Units 1.10.1 to 1.10.7.

Lesson 11
Review of short vowels

Materials: *Explode the Code* Code Cards 1–5

Quick Review

Make sure that every student has Code Cards 1–5 or five index cards with a different vowel on each. Ask the class to listen for the sound they hear in the middle of each of these words and hold up the letter card that matches the sound: *hot, did, get, bud, red, pop, pack, led, cut, sip, pug, jab, Jed, rock, suds, pin, fix, gap, moss, tell, fed, cub,* and *job.*

Phonemic Awareness

Have students tell you the sound they hear in the *middle* of each of these words: *pet, pit, pot, bag, bug, bog, hot, hit, hut, pun, pen, pan, fix, fox,* and *fax.*

Phonics

Skill Review   Play Bingo to review words from Book 1. Give each student a piece of paper with a blank 5" x 5" grid (25 squares). Tell students to put a star in the middle for a free space. Dictate a selection of 24 short-vowel words from Lessons 1–11, telling students to write each word in a square of their choice. Then call out the words you dictated in random order. Tell students to mark each word on their paper as they hear it. The first student who gets five words in a row and has all words spelled correctly is the winner.

Vocabulary

Introduce New Vocabulary   If students are not familiar with lesson words or concepts, provide explanations such as the following: **Pop** is another word for a soft drink. A **well** is a deep hole from which people can get water.

Introduce Sight Words   Introduce the new sight words used in Lesson 11 or the posttest: *of, from,* and *put.* Read the word to the class. Have them think of sentences using the word. Then have them write the letters in the air using their finger as a pencil. Add the sight word to the Word Wall or have students add it to their personal dictionaries.

Completing Student Pages 85–92

Read the directions with students. Identify any pictures that may be unfamiliar, such as *well* and *lock* in row 4 on page 87, and *duck* on page 88. Together, complete a sample item on each page. Then have students complete the pages independently, providing assistance as needed.

Fluency

Read with Expression   Write the following sentences on the board. Point to the first sentence and read it aloud. Have the class echo it by reading it back to you. Then reread all three sentences together:

1. The hot pot has no top.
2. The kid begs Dad to get him a hot dog.
3. The cat has a red bell on its neck.

Comprehension

Write words from Lessons 1–11 on individual cards. Have students pick two cards without looking at them and then make up an oral sentence using the words on the cards. Repeat until all cards have been selected.

Writing   Have students copy the sentences from the fluency exercise onto sheets of lined paper. Remind them to use capital letters at the beginning and periods at the end of each sentence.

Differentiating Instruction

Learning Style (Visual/Kinesthetic)   Create word card sets with these words: *hat, Meg, bid, pot, tug, man, hen, bog, pup, bag, bet, hit, mop, bun, mud, hot, pit, pen, pat, tap, Ted, tin, tot,* and *hut.* Have students sort the cards three times: first by short vowel, next by first letter, and then by final letter. Have them read each new group of words.

Extra Practice   Find more practice with all short vowels in Lesson 11 of *Explode The Code* Book 1½.

Challenge   Have students write the following lengthwise headings across a piece of paper: *-ap, -ip, -up,* and *-op.* Ask them to write as many words as they can under each heading without looking at their books.

Computer-based Reinforcement   Give students additional practice with short vowel review on *ETC Online,* Units 1.11.2 to 1.11.6.

Book 1 Posttest

page 93 Give the instruction, "Circle the word you hear," and dictate the words listed below. The students circle the correct word from a choice of three words.

1. hog
2. web
3. hill
4. cop
5. bad
6. bug
7. him
8. met

page 94 Students write sentences dictated by the teacher. Dictate each sentence slowly once or twice. It is often helpful for the students to repeat each sentence before they write it.

1. Pam hid in a tub.
2. The bug had fun.
3. Bob has a pet.
4. A hen is in bed.
5. Can Mom run? (optional)

page 95 Students complete this page on their own. Simple directions appear at the top of the page. Students choose and circle the word that best completes the sentence.

1. run
2. cup
3. hot
4. rip
5. log
6. bed

page 96 Students complete this page on their own. Simple directions appear at the top of the page. Students read two short paragraphs and select a word to complete each riddle.

1. pup
2. pot

Posttest Book 1½

page 89 Give the instruction, "Circle the word you hear," and dictate the words listed below. Students circle the correct word from a choice of three words.

1. cut
2. sad
3. bib
4. sap
5. wig
6. den
7. hop
8. mud

page 90 Students write sentences dictated by the teacher. Dictate each sentence slowly once or twice. It is often helpful for students to repeat each sentence before they write it.

1. The mat has a big rip.
2. Pam can cut the logs.
3. The cub will nap on the bed.
4. Don gets a tan in the sun.
5. I can run and win a cup.

page 91 Students complete this page on their own. Simple directions appear at the top of the page. Students choose and circle the word that best completes the sentence.

1. wag
2. bus
3. cup
4. dots
5. pup
6. net

page 92 Students complete this page on their own. Simple directions appear at the top of the page. Students read three short paragraphs and select a word to complete each riddle.

1. sun
2. pin
3. tub

Book 2

Lesson 1
Initial consonant blends *bl, cl, fl, gl*

Materials: *Explode the Code* Code Cards 1–9

Quick Review

Provide students with Code Cards 1–5 or five index cards with a different vowel on each. Say the following words and have students display the vowel each word begins with: *apple, igloo, umbrella, octopus, egg, edge, itch, up, ox, egg, odd, us, inch, ask,* and *elk.* Then have students display the vowel in the *middle* of each word you say: *cat, bit, cop, cup, man, hug, pet, pit,* and *net.*

Phonemic Awareness

Phoneme Segmentation   Have students break each of these words into its separate sounds, saying each sound as they tap it out or count it:

lad: /l/ /a/ /d/ (3 sounds)
glad: /g/ /l/ /a/ /d/ (4 sounds)
clap: /c/ /l/ /a/ /p/ (4 sounds)
led: /l/ /e/ /d/ (3 sounds)
fled: /f/ /l/ /e/ /d/ (4 sounds)
black: /b/ /l/ /a/ /k/ (4 sounds)

Phonics

Introduce the Skill   Show students a flower or a picture of a flower and ask them to name it. Display the word *flower* and underline the initial blend. Tell students that sounds of *f* and *l* blend together to say /fl/ as in *flower.* Explain to students that when two consonant sounds are blended together quickly, they are called **blends.**

Write the letters *fl* on a chart or display Code Card 6. Have students brainstorm other words that begin with *fl.* Display some of these words, sounding each letter out as you write it. Then ask volunteers to underline the *fl* blend in each.

Repeat the same process for blends *bl, cl,* and *gl:*

bl block (Code Card 7)
cl clock (Code Card 8)
gl glass (Code Card 9)

Vocabulary

Introduce New Vocabulary   If students are not familiar with lesson words or concepts, provide explanations such as the following: **Clip** is a short way to say paper clip. A **cub** (in this lesson) is a baby bear. A **flat** tire is a tire that has lost its air.

Introduce Sight Words   Introduce the new sight words used in the lesson: *the, is, of, has, or, no, put,* and *you.* Read each word to the class. Have students think of sentences using each word. Then have them write the letters in the air using their fingers as a pencil. Add the sight words to the Word Wall and have students add them to their personal dictionaries.

Completing Student Pages 1–9

Read the directions with students. Identify any pictures that may be unfamiliar. Together, complete a sample item on each page. Then have students complete the pages independently, providing assistance as needed.

Fluency

Word Automaticity   Provide or have students create several flashcards with *bl, gl, cl,* and *fl* words from this lesson. Have students flip through the cards as they read the words to a partner. Students should be encouraged to review the flashcards multiple times as they work to increase their accuracy and speed.

Comprehension

Explain that a sentence must have a subject, a person or thing, and that the subject must do something. Using some simple oral sentences as examples (*kids run; birds fly*), ask students, What is the subject? What do the kids do? Display a word from the lesson. Have volunteers use the word in an oral sentence. Remind them that in a sentence a person or thing must do something. Example: The **flag** flaps in the breeze.

Writing   Write the blends *fl, cl,* and *gl* on the board. Have students write numbers 1–5 on a piece of paper and write a *fl, cl,* or *gl* word from the lesson for each clue you give:

1. Each country has a different one of these colorful banners. (flags)
2. A bird does this with its wings. (flap)
3. If you are in the audience at a school play, you might do this at the end. (clap)
4. What color is the opposite of white? (black)
5. What are windows usually made out of? (glass)

Differentiating Instruction

ELL   Pronunciation of *l* blends may be difficult for native speakers of several Asian languages. See *Explode The Code for English Language Learners* for more work with blends.

Learning Style (Auditory/Kinesthetic)   Give each student a card with a *bl, gl, cl,* or *fl* word from the lesson. Tell students to read the word on the card and say the word aloud as they walk around the room. Have students circulate throughout the room, listening to each other's words. Tell them to join hands with students whose words begin with the same blends. Once all groups have formed, have students in each group say their words aloud. Ask a volunteer from each group to name the blend.

Extra Practice   Find more practice with initial consonant blends *bl, gl, cl,* and *fl* in Lesson 1 of *Explode The Code* Book 2½.

Computer-based Reinforcement   Give students additional practice with initial consonant blends *bl, cl, fl,* and *gl* on *ETC Online*, Units 2.1.2 to 2.1.7.

Lesson 2
Initial consonant blends *sk, sl, pl*

Materials: *Explode the Code* Code Cards 10–12

Quick Review

Have students name the sound and letters of the initial blend in each of the following words: *black, clam, flag, glass, glue, blend, click, glad, floss, class, flick,* and *bless.*

Phonemic Awareness

Phoneme Addition   Ask students the following questions. Students are asked to add a beginning sound to each word to make a new word:

1. What word do you have if you add /p/ to the beginning of *lug*? (plug)
2. What word do you have if you add /p/ to the beginning of *lot*? (plot)
3. If you add /s/ to *led*? (sled)
4. If you add /s/ to *lap*? (slap)
5. If you add /s/ to *lip*? (slip)
6. If you add /s/ to *kid*? (skid)
7. If you add /s/ to *kin*? (skin)

Phonics

Introduce the Skill   Show students a plug or a picture of a plug and ask them to name it. Display the word *plug* and underline the initial blend. Tell students that sounds of *p* and *l* blend together to say /pl/ as in *plug*.

Write the letters *pl* on a chart or display Code Card 10. Have students brainstorm other words that begin with *pl.* Display some of these words and ask volunteers to underline the *pl* blend in each word.

Repeat the same process for blends *sk* and *sl:*

sk, skate (Code Card 11)
sl, sled (Code Card 12)

Vocabulary

Introduce New Vocabulary   If students are not familiar with lesson words or concepts, provide explanations such as the following: To **skid** means to slide without being able to stop. A car might **skid** on a wet road. A **club** can be a place where people get together. **Slim** means thin.

Introduce Sight Words   Introduce the new sight words used in the lesson: *off* and *his.* Read each word to the class. Have students think of sentences using each word. Then have them write the letters in the air using their fingers as a pencil. Add the sight words to the Word Wall and have students add them to their personal dictionaries.

Completing Student Pages 10–18

Read the directions with students. Identify any pictures that may be unfamiliar, such as *plum* in row 1 and *skip* in row 4 on page 12; and *skid* on row 4 on page 13. Together, complete a sample item on each page. Then have students complete the pages independently, providing assistance as needed.

Fluency

Noting Punctuation   Display the following text on the board and/or make copies for each student. Remind students to pause at the periods when they read. Remind them that exclamation marks tell you to speak with excitement. Model reading the passage for the students. Then have student read the passage. Note whether they are observing punctuation marks as they read.

Fluff the cat sat on a red sled.
The red sled slid and slid.
O! O! O!
The red sled skids.
O! O! O!
Fluff slips off.
Plop!

Comprehension

Extending Word Knowledge   Say each highlighted word. Then read the following sentences and have students tell you what the word means in each sentence:

1. **skim:** I will **skim** the book to find out what happens at the end. (read quickly)
2. **skim:** She can throw the rocks so they **skim** across the water.
   (to glide across the top of)
3. **skin:** Peel the **skin** before you eat the apple.
   (the peel, or the outer part, of a fruit or vegetable)
4. **skin:** Lotion makes my **skin** softer. (outer part of the body)
5. **skip:** I had to **skip** the soccer meet when I was sick.
   (having to miss something; not going)
6. **skip:** The two friends hold hands and **skip.** (hop)

Writing   Have students copy the following sentences onto lined sheets of paper and complete them with their own words.

1. I slid on a _____.
2. Glen will dig and _____.
3. A black bug is on _____.
4. I will skip to the _____.
5. Ten plus ten is _____.

Differentiating Instruction

Learning Style (Visual/Kinesthetic)   Provide visual/kinesthetic learners with word cards with *sl, sk,* and *pl* words from the lesson. Have students sort the words according to their beginning blends. Once they have sorted the words into three groups, have them read the words in each group aloud.

Challenge   Have students make up word equations such as the following:

skip - p + n = (skin)
plum - m + g = (plug)
step - ep + ill = (still)
slop - op + ed = (sled)

ELL   See *Explode The Code for English Language Learners* for more work with blends.

Computer-based Reinforcement   Give students additional practice with initial consonant blends *sk, sl,* and *pl* on *ETC Online,* Units 2.2.2 to 2.2.8.

Lesson 3
Initial consonant blends *cr, dr, gr*

Materials: *Explode the Code* Code Cards 10–12 and 13–15

Quick Review
Provide students with Code Cards 10–12 or cards with the blends *sk, sl,* and *pl.* Have students listen carefully to the following words and hold up the card that matches the initial blend: *plop, slug, skid, plan, plunder, skipping, sloppy, slipper, skunk,* and *plaster.*

Phonemic Awareness
Phoneme Identity   Ask students which beginning sounds the following sets of words have in common:

    crown, cricket, crush (/kr/)
    droop, drink, drive (/dr/)
    grip, great, ground (/gr/)
    crate, crow, crab (/kr/)
    drain, drag, Drake (/dr/)
    group, grow, gravel (/gr/)

Phonics
Introduce the Skill   Show students a crown or a picture of a crown and ask them to name it. Display the word *crown* and underline the initial blend. Tell students that sounds of *c* and *r* blend together to say /kr/ as in *crown.*

Write the letters *cr* on a chart or display Code Card 13. Have students brainstorm other words that begin with *cr.* Display some of these words, and ask volunteers to underline the *cr* blend in each word.

Repeat the same process for blends *dr* and *gr:*

    dr, dragon (Code Card 14)
    gr, grapes (Code Card 15)

Vocabulary
Introduce New Vocabulary   If students are not familiar with lesson words or concepts, provide explanations such as the following: **Grin** is another word for smile. A **crib** is a bed for a baby. To **grill** means to cook over a fire.

Introduce Sight Words   Introduce the new sight word used in the lesson: *and.* Read the word to the class. Have them think of sentences using this word. Then have them write the letters in the air using their fingers as a pencil. Add the sight word to the Word Wall and have students add it to their personal dictionaries.

Completing Student Pages 19–27

Read the directions with students. Identify any pictures that may be unfamiliar, such as the *cross* (which looks like a plus sign) on page 21. Together, complete a sample item on each page. Then have students complete the pages independently, providing assistance as needed.

Fluency

Reading Dialogue   Write the following text on the board or an overhead. Point out that quotation marks indicate that someone is speaking. Remind students to read dialogue as a character might say it. They can practice this fluency skill by reading the passage aloud.

> The crab has a plan.
> "Black bug! Black bug!
> Let's skip in the grass!"
>
> The crab has a grin.
> "Black bug! Black bug!
> Let's slip in the mud!"
>
> But the black bug ran
> and hid in a crack.

Comprehension

Extending Word Knowledge   Say each highlighted word. Then read the following sentences and have students tell you what the highlighted word means in each sentence:

1. **drop:** I felt a **drop** of water from the sky. (a drip or droplet)
2. **drop:** Try not to **drop** the glass vase. (let fall)
3. **dress:** On school picture day, she wore a pretty **dress**. (clothing)
4. **dress:** I will **dress** for school and then eat my breakfast. (put on clothes)
5. **dragged:** The movie **dragged** on and on and I got tired. (moved slowly)
6. **dragged:** My dad **dragged** a box of decorations from the closet. (pulled out)

Writing   Have students copy the following sentences onto sheets of lined paper. Challenge them to use one of the sentences as a story starter and write a short story.

   1. The crab sits on a log.
   2. I get a hit, drop the bat in the grass, and run!

Differentiating Instruction

ELL   Note that pronunciation of blends that include the letter *r* may be especially difficult for native speakers of some Asian languages. See *Explode The Code for English Language Learners* for more work with blends.

Learning Style (Visual)   Visual learners may enjoy creating a word web of *cr* (or *gr* or *dr*) words arranged around the letters *cr* (or *gr* or *dr*) in the center.

Challenge   Students who complete these pages without difficulty can create clues for lesson words and share the clues with a partner. For example, *It is red, has claws, and likes the water.* (crab)

Computer-based Reinforcement   Give students additional practice with initial consonant blends *cr, dr,* and *gr* on *ETC Online,* Units 2.3.2 to 2.3.8.

Lesson 4
Initial consonant blends *br, fr, pr, tr*

Materials: *Explode the Code* Code Cards 16–19

Quick Review

Review the sounds and key words for blends *cr, dr,* and *gr.* Then ask students if the initial blends in the following pairs of words are the same or different:

   grab, drab (no)
   grass, gross (yes)
   drink, drapes (yes)
   crow, drop (no)
   crock, crutch (yes)
   grow, drive (no)

Phonemic Awareness

Phoneme Blending   Tell students you are going to sound out some words very slowly. Ask students to listen to the sounds and say the word:

/f/ /r/ /e/ /n/ /d/ = friend
/b/ /r/ /a/ /g/ = brag
/t/ /r/ /i/ /m/ = trim
/p/ /r/ /o/ /p/ = prop
/t/ /r/ /a/ /p/ = trap
/f/ /r/ /o/ /g/ = frog

Phonics

Introduce the Skill   Show students some fruit or a picture of fruit and ask them to name it. Display the word *fruit* and underline the initial blend. Tell students that sounds of *f* and *r* blend together to say /fr/ as in *fruit*.

Write the letters *fr* on a chart or display Code Card 16. Have students brainstorm other words that begin with *fr*. Display some of these words and ask volunteers to underline the *fr* blend in each word.

Repeat the same process for blends *br, pr,* and *tr:*

br, broom (Code Card 17)
pr, pretzel (Code Card 18)
tr, tree (Code Card 19)

Vocabulary

Introduce New Vocabulary   If students are not familiar with lesson words or concepts, provide explanations such as the following: **Trim** means the material around the edge of something like a blanket. It can also mean to cut. To **trot** is to move at slow run. A horse sometimes **trots**. A **triangle** is a shape with three sides.

Introduce Sight Words   Introduce the new sight word used in the lesson: *go.* Read the word to the class. Have students think of sentences using this word. Then have them write the letters in the air using their fingers as a pencil. Add the sight word to the Word Wall and have students add it to their personal dictionaries.

Completing Student Pages 28–36

Read the directions with students. Identify any pictures that may be unfamiliar, such as *trap* in row 3 and *press* in row 7 on page 30; and *tap* in row 2 on page 33. Together, complete a sample item on each page. Then have students complete the pages independently, providing assistance as needed.

Fluency

Phrasing Write the following text on the board. Tell students to think about the meanings of words as they read aloud. Tell them that when they read a passage to notice that some words seem to belong together as a group. Model reading the first passage below, paying particular attention to phrasing. Then have students read the second passage aloud a few times. Then have them read the same words in a different format in passage 2.

The Bad Crab, Passage 1
SLAP!
The bad crab
grabs the black bug
and drags him back.
But the black bug
gets mad
and nips the crab
on the back.
The crab
drops the black bug,
The bug is glad, glad, glad!

The Bad Crab, Passage 2
SLAP! The bad crab grabs the black bug and drags him back.
But the black bug gets mad and nips the crab on the back.
The crab drops the black bug. The bug is glad, glad, glad!

Comprehension

Understanding Text Have students draw a picture that shows what happens in "The Bad Crab" story. Review each student's picture and ask him or her to explain it.

Writing Display the blends *tr*, *fr*, and *pr*. Have students write numbers 1–5 on sheets of lined paper. Tell them to choose and write the *tr*, *fr*, or *pr* word that matches each clue.

1. This animal is related to a toad. (frog)
2. This means to cut. (trim)
3. This is another word for a vacation. (trip)
4. A horse does this. (trot)
5. What do you do with a button to go up or down in an elevator? (press)

Differentiating Instruction

Extra Practice Find more practice with initial consonant blends *br*, *cr*, *dr*, *fr*, and *gr* in Lesson 4 of *Explode The Code* Book 2½.

ELL See *Explode The Code for English Language Learners* for more work with blends.

Challenge   Have students identify words from the lesson that have smaller words within them. Then have them write word equations for those words. The equation for the word *trim*, for example, is *t + rim = trim.* Other words may include *trip, trot, trap, track, Fred, Fran,* and *brick.*

Computer-based Reinforcement   Give students additional practice with initial consonant blends *br, fr, pr,* and *tr* on *ETC Online,* Units 2.4.2 to 2.4.8.

Lesson 5

Initial consonant blends *sm, sn, sp*

Materials: a soft ball, *Explode the Code* Code Cards 20–22

Quick Review

Review blends learned thus far: *bl, fl, gl, cl, pl, sk, sl, cr, gr, dr, fr, br, pr,* and *tr.* Throw a soft ball to a student as you say the sound of one of the blends. (/bl/) Have the student name the letters that make that sound (bl) and a word that includes that blend (block).

Phonemic Awareness

Phoneme Segmentation   Have students break each word into its separate sounds, saying each sound as they tap out or count the sounds.

nip: /n/ /i/ /p/ (3 sounds)
snip: /s/ /n/ /i/ /p/ (4 sounds)
smell: /s/ /m/ /e/ /l/ (4 sounds)
pot: /p/ /o/ /t/ (3 sounds)
spot: /s/ /p/ /o/ /t/ (4 sounds)
spill: /s/ /p/ /i/ /l/ (4 sounds)

Phonics

Introduce the Skill   Show students a picture of a snake and ask them to name it. Display the word *snake* and underline the initial blend. Tell students that sounds of *s* and *n* blend together to say /sn/ as in *snake.*

Write the letters *sn* on a chart or display Code Card 20. Have students brainstorm other words that begin with *sn.* Display some of these words and ask volunteers to underline the *sn* blend in each word.

Repeat the same process for blends *sm* and *sp:*

sm, smoke (Code Card 21)
sp, spider (Code Card 22)

Vocabulary

Introduce New Vocabulary   If students are not familiar with lesson words or concepts, provide explanations such as the following: To **snip** means to cut with scissors. To **sniff** means to smell.

Completing Student Pages 37–45

Read the directions with students. Identify any pictures that may be unfamiliar, such as *spill* in the third row on page 37 and *spin* in the fourth row on page 39. Together, complete a sample item on each page. Then have students complete the pages independently, providing assistance as needed.

Fluency

Noting Punctuation   Display the following questions. Remind students to note question marks and when they read aloud to raise the pitch of their voices at the ends of sentences with questions. Model as necessary. Then have pairs of students take turns reading the questions to one another. Monitor for appropriate expression:

1. Will you trip on a brick?
2. Will you trot on a track?
3. Will you trap a big frog?

Comprehension

Extending Word Knowledge   Ask students the following questions about words from the lesson.

1. A top is a toy than **spins** around and around. Name some other things that **spin**. (wheels, tornados, clothes in the dryer)
2. What are some healthy foods that you can eat for a **snack**? (fruits, vegetables)
3. What *sn* word means almost the same as **smell**? (sniff)
4. What *sn* word means almost the same as cut or clip? (snip)

Writing   Have students copy the following sentences onto lined sheets of paper and complete them with words of their own:

1. I did not spill the _____.
2. The cat spots a _____.
3. You can smell a _____.
4. I will snip the _____.

Differentiating Instruction

ELL   In the Spanish language, s-blends never appear at the beginning of words. Letter combinations like *sp* are usually preceded by the letter *e*, as in the word *especial.* Note that Spanish-speaking students may add or omit letters when trying to encode words with these initial blends.

Computer-based Reinforcement   Give students additional practice with initial consonant blends *sm, sn,* and *sp* on *ETC Online,* Units 2.5.2 to 2.5.8.

Lesson 6

Initial consonant blends *st, sw, tw*

Materials: *Explode the Code* Code Cards 23–25

Quick Review

Ask students to name the common initial blend in each set of words:

snoop, snorkel, snap (sn)
smoke, smith, smile (sm)
spoon, sputter, spat (sp)
smudge, small, smock (sm)
spine, sport, spectacle (sp)
snag, snip, snow (sn)

Phonemic Awareness

Phoneme Addition   Have students add a beginning sound to each word to make a new word. Ask students the following questions:

1. What word do you have if you add /s/ to the beginning of *top*? (stop)
2. What word do you have if you add /s/ to the beginning of *tore*? (store)
3. If you add /s/ to *wing*? (swing)
4. If you add /s/ to *weep*? (sweep)
5. If you add /t/ to *wig*? (twig)
6. If you add /t/ to *win*? (twin)

Phonics

Introduce the Skill   Show students a stamp or a picture of a stamp and ask them to name it. Display the word *stamp* and underline the initial blend. Tell students that sounds of *s* and *t* blend together to say /st/ as in *stamp.*

Write the letters *st* on a chart or display Code Card 23. Have students brainstorm other words that begin with *st*. Display some of these words and ask volunteers to underline the *st* blend in each word.

Repeat the same process for blends *sw* and *tw:*

sw, swing (Code Card 24)
tw, twig (Code Card 25)

Vocabulary

Introduce New Vocabulary   If students are not familiar with lesson words or concepts, provide explanations such as the following: A **stem** is part of a flower. A **stack** is a pile; to **stack** means to make a pile.

Introduce Sight Words   Introduce the new sight words used in the lesson: *to* and *swan.* Read each word to the class. Have students think of sentences using each word. Then have them write the letters in the air using their fingers as a pencil. Add the sight words to the Word Wall or have students add them to their personal dictionaries.

Completing Student Pages 46–54

Read the directions with students. Identify any pictures that may be unfamiliar, such as *twig* in row 3 and *stuck* in row 6 on page 48. Together, complete a sample item on each page. Then have students complete the pages independently, providing assistance as needed.

Fluency

Developing Accuracy   Have students reread the sentences on page 53 aloud with a partner. Challenge the students to read the sentences rapidly and accurately.

Comprehension

Extending Word Knowledge   Have students answer the following questions about words from the lesson:

1. What is another word for *double* or *look-alike*? (twin)
2. What is another word for *stick* or *branch*? (twig)
3. What is ten plus ten? (twenty)
4. Name the missing part of the flower: petals, leaves, and _____. (stem)
5. What is the opposite of *go*? (stop)
6. What is the opposite of *moving*? (still)

Writing Have students choose two questions from page 52 and copy them onto sheets of lined paper. Remind them to use a capital letter at the beginning of each question and a question mark at the end. Then have them write an answer to the question in a complete sentence, using a capital letter at the beginning and a period at the end.

Differentiating Instruction

Learning Style (Visual) Visual learners may enjoy creating a word web of *st* (or *sw* or *tw*) words arranged around the letters *st* (or *sw* or *tw*) in the center.

Challenge Have students identify words from the lesson that have smaller words within them. Then have them write word equations for those words. The equation for the word *stop,* for example, is *s + top = stop.* Other words may include *stuck, twin, spin, twig,* and *stick.*

Extra Practice Find more practice with these initial consonant blends in *Explode The Code* Book 2½.

Computer-based Reinforcement Give students additional practice with initial consonant blends *st, sw,* and *tw* on *ETC Online,* Units 2.6.2 to 2.6.8.

Lesson 7
Review Lesson: Initial Consonant Blends

Materials: *Explode the Code* Code Cards 23–25

Quick Review

Use Code Cards 23–25 or make cards with initial blends *st, sw,* and *tw.* Show the cards one at a time and ask volunteers to name the initial blend, give its sound, and provide two words with that blend. For example, *st* says /st/ as in *stop* and *stick.*

Phonemic Awareness

Ask students to listen carefully to the following words. Tell them to point their thumbs up if the word begins with a blend and down if the word does not begin with a blend: *grapes, smile, rack, braid, stack, test, planet, snort, click, space, flop, dock, sweet,* and *trickle.*

Phonics

Skill Review   Have students listen to each pair of words and name the common initial blend. Have students name the *letters,* not the sound. Challenge students to come up with another word that begins with the same blend:

black, block *(bl)*
drop, drag *(dr)*
sled, slam *(sl)*
twin, twig *(tw)*
stick, step *(st)*
trap, trot *(tr)*
flip, flat *(fl)*
click, clap *(cl)*
smell, smile *(sm)*

Vocabulary

Introduce New Vocabulary   If students are not familiar with lesson words or concepts, provide explanations as necessary.

Introduce Sight Words   Introduce the new sight words used in the lesson: *he* and *be.* Read each word to the class. Have them think of sentences using each word. Then have them write the letters in the air using their fingers as a pencil. Add the sight words to the Word Wall or have students add them to their personal dictionaries.

Completing Student Pages 55–60

Read the directions with students. Identify any pictures that may be unfamiliar. Together, complete a sample item on each page. Then have students complete the pages independently, providing assistance as needed.

Fluency

Read with Expression   Have students reread the questions on page 58 with a partner. Monitor for appropriate expression.

Comprehension

Have students draw a picture to illustrate one of the following words: **grin, slam, smell, drop, trip,** and **trot.** Have students label their pictures with the word and share with the rest of the class why they drew the picture the way they did.

Writing   Have students copy the following sentences onto sheets of lined paper to complete with words of their own. Have them underline all the words that have initial consonant blends.

1. The twin will spin the _____.
2. A frog stops and sits still on a _____.
3. If you trip on the step you will _____.
4. The dog will swim to get the _____.
5. Did you get stuck in the _____?

Differentiating Instruction

Challenge   Have students write alliterative phrases or sentences using at least three words with the same initial blend. Encourage students to sound out any words that they are not sure how to spell. For example: The crab cries in the crib. I plan to plant a plum tree.

ELL   Have students pantomime words from various lessons and have other students guess the word. Provide the initial blend as a clue if necessary.

Computer-based Reinforcement   Give students additional practice with initial consonant blend review on *ETC Online,* Units 2.7.2 to 2.7.4.

Lesson 8

Final consonant blends -*mp, -sk, -st*

Materials: *Explode the Code* Code Cards 26–28

Quick Review

Ask students to name some of the initial blends learned in lessons 1–7 and write those blends in columns across the board. Ask volunteers to name words that fall under each heading and write the words in the appropriate columns. When you have a good list, read the words aloud with the class. Tell students that today they will be learning words that have *final* blends.

Phonemic Awareness

Phoneme Blending   Tell students you are going to sound out some words very slowly. Ask students to listen to the sounds and say each word:

/t/ /e/ /s/ /t/ = test
/p/ /a/ /s/ /t/ = past
/l/ /o/ /s/ /t/ = lost
/d/ /e/ /s/ /k/ = desk
/t/ /a/ /s/ /k/ = task
/l/ /i/ /m/ /p/ = limp
/b/ /u/ /m/ /p/ = bump

Phonics

Introduce the Skill   Show students a nest or a picture of a nest and ask them to name it. Display the word *nest* and underline the final blend. Tell students that sounds of *s* and *t* blend together at the end of a word to say /st/ as in *nest.*

Write the letters *-st* on a chart or display Code Card 26. Have students work with word families like *-est* (*nest, best, rest, test,* and *vest*); *-ast* (*last, past,* and *cast*); and *-ust* (*must, just, dust,* and *rust*) to brainstorm other words that end with *-st.* Display some of these words, sounding them out as you write them. Then ask volunteers to underline the final *-st* blend in each word.

Repeat the same process for final blends *-sk* and *-mp:*

-sk, mask (Code Card 27)
-mp, lamp (Code Card 28)

Vocabulary

Introduce New Vocabulary   If students are not familiar with lesson words or concepts, provide explanations such as the following: To **camp** means to stay in a temporary shelter. You put a **cast** on a broken arm to protect it and help it heal. A **hump** is a bump on a camel's back.

Completing Student Pages 60–68

Read the directions with students. Identify any pictures that may be unfamiliar, such as *mask* and *pump* on page 60 and *last, vest, fist,* and *ask* on page 62. Together, complete a sample item on each page. Then have students complete the pages independently, providing assistance as needed.

Fluency

Improving Rate   Have students chorally read the sentences on page 67. Guide them by setting a pace that allows them to pronounce the words clearly and quickly. Then point out and read various sentences at a slightly faster pace.

Comprehension

Extending Word Knowledge   Have students answer the following clues with *-st, -mp,* or *-sk* words from the lesson:

1. This is what birds call home. (nest)
2. If you break your arm, you will probably have to get one of these. (cast)
3. You might wear one of these if you dress up in a costume. (mask)

4. If you are at the end of a line, you are not first. You are what? (last)

5. This is something you turn on when you want read a book at night. (lamp)

6. This is a name for a sweater with no sleeves. (vest)

7. This word means "hop, skip, or leap." (jump)

8. If you have a question, what do you do with it? (ask)

Writing   Dictate three questions from page 66 and have students copy them onto a sheet of lined paper. Remind them to use a capital letter at the beginning of each question and a question mark at the end. Then have students write a question of their own. Encourage them to include -st, -mp, or -sk words from the lesson.

Differentiating Instruction

ELL   See *Explode The Code for English Language Learners* for more work with blends.

Learning Style (Kinesthetic)   Provide kinesthetic learners with word cards with several -st, -mp, and -sk words from the lesson. Have students sort the words according to their final blends. Once they have sorted the words into three groups, have them read aloud the words in each group.

Challenge   Challenge students to add an initial consonant to each of the following words to make a new word (answers in parentheses): *lamp* (clamp), *last* (blast), *ask* (task, mask, or bask), *rust* (crust or trust), *ramp* (cramp), *limp* (blimp), and *lump* (plump or clump).

Computer-based Reinforcement   Give students additional practice with final consonant blends -mp, -sk, and -st on *ETC Online*, Units 2.8.2 to 2.8.8.

Lesson 9

Final consonant blends *-ft, -lt, -nt*

Materials: *Explode The Code* Cards 29–31

Quick Review

Provide students with letter tiles or a white board. Tell students to build or write the word *fast.* Then tell students they will be adding, removing, or substituting one letter to make a new word. Tell them to change *fast* to *last.* Monitor for understanding of the task, then continue with the following words: *mast, mask, bask, ask, as, at, cat, cap, camp,* and *clamp.*

Phonemic Awareness

Phoneme Segmentation   Have students break each word into its separate sounds, saying each sound as they tap it out or count it:

ant: /a/ /n/ /t/ (3 sounds)
mint: /m/ /i/ /n/ /t/ (4 sounds)
spent: /s/ /p/ /e/ /n/ /t/ (5 sounds)
wilt: /w/ /i/ /l/ /t/ (4 sounds)
melt: /m/ /e/ /l/ /t/ (4 sounds)
lift: /l/ /i/ /f/ /t/ (4 sounds)
craft: /k/ /r/ /a/ /f/ /t/ (5 sounds)

Phonics

Introduce the Skill   Show students a picture of a tent and ask them to name it. Display the word *tent* and underline the final blend. Tell students that sounds of *n* and *t* blend together at the end of a word to say /nt/ as in *tent.*

Write the letters *-nt* on a chart or display Code Card 29. Have students work with word families like *-ent* (*tent, bent, sent, rent,* and *went*) and *-int* (*hint, lint, mint,* and *tint*) to brainstorm other words that end with *-nt.* Display some of these words and then ask volunteers to underline the final *-nt* blend in each word.

Repeat the same process for final blends *-lt* and *-ft:*

-lt, belt (Code Card 30)
-ft, gift (Code Card 31)

Vocabulary

Introduce New Vocabulary   If students are not familiar with lesson words or concepts, provide explanations such as the following: A **raft** is a floating structure that is used like a boat. It is made of boards or logs fastened together.

Completing Student Pages 69–77

Read the directions with students. Identify any pictures that may be unfamiliar, such as *lift, melt, plant,* and *raft* on page 69; *hunt* on page 71; and *sent* on page 72. Together, complete a sample item on each page. Then have students complete the pages independently, providing assistance as needed.

Fluency

Word Automaticity   Provide or have students create several flashcards with *-nt, -lt,* and *-ft* words from this lesson. You may also choose to include other final blend words from earlier lessons. Have students flip through the cards as they read the words to a partner. Students should be encouraged to review the flashcards multiple times as they work to increase their accuracy and speed.

Comprehension

Extending Word Knowledge   Have students answer the following questions about words from the lesson:

1. Name some things that might **melt**. (ice, ice cream, chocolate, snow)
2. What is a word that means the same as **gift**? (present)
3. There are different kinds of **tents**. Where might you see different kinds of tents? (a campground, circus, or fair)

Writing   Dictate four sentences from page 76 and have students write the sentences on sheets of lined paper. Remind students to use capital letters and periods.

Differentiating Instruction

Learning Style (Auditory)   Have auditory learners think of some words that rhyme with *ant*. As students think of words, write them on the board. When you have a good collection, ask the class to read them aloud together. Then ask them to provide some oral sentences or rhymes using these words, for example, *The ant crawled up the plant.*

Challenge   If students complete these pages without difficulty, have them work with inflected verb endings. Ask students to add the endings *-s, -ed,* and *-ing* to the verbs *melt* and *lift* and to use each form of the verb in a sentence. Encourage students to sound out any words that they are not sure how to spell. For example: *The snow melts in the sun. The ice melted when the sun came out. The candy is melting in my hands!*

Extra Practice   Find more practice with these final consonant blends in *Explode The Code* Book 2½.

Computer-based Reinforcement   Give students additional practice with final consonant blends *-ft, -lt,* and *-nt* on *ETC Online,* Units 2.9.2 to 2.9.8.

Lesson 10
Final consonant blends -*lf, -lp, -nd, -nk*

Materials: *Explode the Code* Code Cards 29–35

Quick Review

Provide students with Code Cards 29–31 or other cards displaying the *-ft, -nt,* and *-lt* blends. Tell students to listen to the end of each word. Ask them to display the card with the blend they hear at the end of the following words: *sift, pant, hint, felt, gift, left, went,* and *belt.*

Phonemic Awareness

Phoneme Substitution   Have students say the word *hand*. Then ask students to change the /h/ to a /b/ and say the new word (*band*). Continue substituting initial sounds as students build the following sets of words:

> hand, band, sand, land
> bend, tend, send, mend
> wink, pink, link, sink
> tank, sank, bank, yank

Phonics

Introduce the Skill   Show students your hand or a picture of a hand and ask them to name it. Display the word *hand* and underline the final blend. Tell students that sounds of *n* and *d* blend together at the end of a word to say /nd/ as in *hand*.

Write the letters *-nd* on a chart or display Code Card 32. Have students work with word families like *-and* (*hand, band, sand,* and *land*) and *-end* (*end, send, bend, tend, lend,* and *mend*) to brainstorm other words that end with *-nd*. Display some of these words. Then ask volunteers to underline the final *-nd* blend in each word.

Repeat the same process for final blends *-nk, -lp,* and *-lf:*

> *-nk,* wink (Code Card 33)
> *-lp,* gulp (Code Card 34)
> *-lf,* elf (Code Card 35)

Vocabulary

Introduce New Vocabulary   If students are not familiar with lesson words or concepts, provide explanations as necessary. For example, if you **wink** you close one eye. **Golf** is a sport played with clubs and a small, hard ball; the goal is to hit the ball into a series of holes.

Completing Student Pages 78–86

Read the directions with students. Identify any pictures that may be unfamiliar, such as *elf* on page 78, *ink* and *pond* on page 81, and *spend* on page 87. Together, complete a sample item on each page. Then have students complete the pages independently, providing assistance as needed.

Fluency

Read with Expression   Display the following four passages. Make sure students can read the sight words *he* and *her*. Divide students into two groups for a choral reading activity. Have each group read alternate passages. Then have groups switch passages and read again. Then have all the students read the four passages together with expression.

Tess fills the glass of milk.
Tess spills the glass of milk.
Tess has a big mess.

So Tess gets a wet, wet mop
and slops and slops and slops.
"Stop!" yells Pops. "Stop! Stop!"

Pops grabs the mop.
He tells Tess he will fix the mess.
Tess drops the mop and has a rest.

Pops mops up the mess. Bless Pops!
Tess has no mess to mop.
Her Pops is tops!

Comprehension

Extending Word Knowledge Ask students to tell you what the highlighted word means in each sentence.

1. We walked along the beach in the **sand**. (fine, loose grains of rock/quartz)
2. **Sand** the rough spots on the chair before you paint it. (smooth)
3. I put my dirty dishes in the **sink**. (a basin with a faucet)
4. The rock will **sink** if you throw it into the water. (go below the surface)

Writing Have students write three original questions, using two -nd, -nk, -lp, or -lf words from the lesson in each sentence. Provide the following example, underlining the lesson words: *Can you lend me a hand?*

Differentiating Instruction

Extra Practice Find more practice with -nd, -nk, -lp, and -lf in Lessons 7 and 8 of *Explode The Code* Book 2½.

Learning Style (Visual) Have students trace an outline of a hand in the middle of a piece of paper and write *hand* inside the outline. Have them write the *h* in one color and the *and* in another. Then have students write other -and words around the hand, again using a different color for the *and* in each word. Answers may include *land, band, sand, stand, grand, brand,* and *bland.* (Words with both initial and final blends are presented in Lesson 11.)

Computer-based Reinforcement Give students additional practice with final consonant blends -lf, -lp, -nd, and -nk on *ETC Online*, Units 2.10.2 to 2.10.8.

Lesson 11
Review Lesson: Initial and final consonant blends

Quick Review

Have students use letter tiles or a white board to build or write the following sequence of words: *ink, link, wink, win, tin, ten, tend, lend, send,* and *bend.*

Phonemic Awareness

Have students add a beginning sound to each word to make a new word. Ask students the following questions:

1. What word do you have if you add /k/ to the beginning of *rest*? (crest)
2. What word do you have if you add /s/ to the beginning of *wept*? (swept)
3. If you add /k/ to *lamp*? (clamp)
4. If you add /s/ to *lick*? (slick)
5. If you add /b/ to *link*? (blink)
6. If you add /t/ to *win*? (twin)
7. If you add /b/ to *last*? (blast)

Phonics

Skill Review   Remind students that they have learned many words with initial blends and many words with final blends. Tell students that in this lesson they will be working with words that have *both* an initial and a final blend.

Display the following list of words: *stink, bent, crest, stop, twist, grand, just, spent, pump, swim, crib, plump, hint,* and *trust.* Ask volunteers to look at a word and tell you whether the word has an initial blend, a final blend, or both. Have them underline the blend or blends and read the word.

Vocabulary

Introduce New Vocabulary   If students are not familiar with lesson words or concepts, provide explanations as necessary. For example, a **dent** is an indentation on a surface, like a **dent** on a car. If someone is **cross,** he or she is angry. When something **sinks** in liquid, it goes under the surface.

Introduce Sight Words   Introduce the new sight words used in the posttest: *from* and *do*. Read each word to the class. Have students think of sentences using each word. Then have them write the letters in the air using their fingers as a pencil. Add the sight words to the Word Wall or have students add them to their personal dictionaries.

Completing Student Pages 87–91
Read the directions with students. Identify any pictures that may be unfamiliar, such as *crust* and *twist* on page 87. Together, complete a sample item on each page. Then have students complete the pages independently, providing assistance as needed.

Fluency
Developing Accuracy   Have students reread the sentences on pages 90 aloud with a partner. Challenge the students to read the sentences rapidly yet accurately. For additional practice, students may also reread the sentences on pages 67, 76, and 85.

Comprehension
Extending Word Knowledge   Ask students to tell you what each highlighted word means in the sentence.

1. The elephant picked up peanuts with its **trunk.** (the long "nose" of an elephant)
2. I packed clothes in a **trunk** for the long trip. (chest or box)
3. You will need a **stamp** to send that letter. (postage for the mail)
4. He will **stamp** my hand to show that I have paid. (mark)
5. I'll have to **stand** up to see the pictures in the book. (get up, rise)
6. I can't **stand** loud music! (put up with, take)

Writing   Dictate the following sentences and have students write the sentences on lined sheets of paper. Remind students to use capital letters and periods.

1. A kid sent a frog to his mom as a gift.
2. A skunk crept in a tent at camp.
3. The kids jump and skip and clap hands.

Differentiating Instruction
Extra Practice   Find more practice with initial and final blends in Lessons 10–12 of *Explode The Code* Book 2½.

ELL   See *Explode The Code for English Language Learners* for more work with blends.

Learning Style (Kinesthetic)   Provide kinesthetic learners with letter tiles or a white board. Tell students to build or write the word *ant.* Then tell students they will be adding, removing, or substituting one letter to make a new word. Tell them to change *ant* to *pant.* Monitor for understanding of the task, then continue with the following words: *plant, plan, pan, pen, pent, rent, runt, hunt,* and *hut.*

Computer-based Reinforcement   Give students additional practice with consonant blends on *ETC Online,* Units 2.11.1 to 2.11.4.

Book 2 Posttest

page 92 Give the instruction, "Circle the word you hear," and dictate the words listed below. The students circle the correct word from a choice of three words.

1. blink
2. crust
3. swept
4. stand
5. held
6. drink
7. grant
8. spend
9. trust
10. left

page 93 Students write sentences dictated by the teacher. Dictate each sentence slowly once or twice. It is often helpful for the students to repeat each sentence before they write it.

1. A truck can stop fast.
2. Brad hunts in the grass.
3. Kim must drink milk.
4. Fred slid on his sled.
5. The crab has a flag. (optional)

page 94 Students complete this page on their own. Students read four short paragraphs and add the correct letters to complete the final word of each paragraph.

1. frog
2. plant
3. milk
4. tent

Posttest Book 2½

page 103 Give the instruction, "Circle the word you hear," and dictate the words listed below. The students circle the correct word from a choice of four words.

1. bland
2. skimp
3. slump
4. draft
5. blank
6. clamp
7. trust
8. crisp

page 104 Students write sentences dictated by the teacher. Dictate each sentence slowly once or twice. It is often helpful for the students to repeat the sentence before they write it.

1. Clem picks the best plum.
2. Fran held up a silk flag.
3. The elk has a black belt.
4. Will you flunk the test?
5. Frank has a blond wig.
6. Babs is grand at the rink.

page 105 Students complete this page on their own. Simple directions are included at the top of the page. Students read four short paragraphs and add the correct letters to complete the final word of each paragraph.

1. golf
2. truck
3. camp
4. crab

page 106 Students complete this page on their own. Students choose one word that best completes each sentence. Choices are listed at the top of the page.

1. plant
2. song
3. winks
4. drink
5. pranks
6. clasps